DISCOVER
The Renaissance in Italy

by Vickey Herold

Table of Contents

Introduction	2
Chapter 1 What Was the Renaissance in Italy?	4
Chapter 2 What Were the Changes in Italy?	8
Chapter 3 What Was Life Like in Italy?	14
Conclusion	18
Concept Map	20
Glossary	22
Index	24

Introduction

The Renaissance was a time in history. The Renaissance was in **Italy**. The Renaissance was a time for change.

▲ The Renaissance was in Italy.

Words to Know

 art

 city-states

 Italy

 literature

 the Renaissance

 wars

See the Glossary on page 22.

Chapter 1

What Was the Renaissance in Italy?

The Renaissance was a time in Italy.

▲ The Renaissance was in Italy.

It's a Fact

The Renaissance began in Italy. The Renaissance began about 1400 A.D.

The Renaissance was a time to study. The Renaissance was a time to learn.

▲ The Renaissance had learning.

Chapter 1

The Renaissance was a time for ideas. The Renaissance was a time for **literature**.

▲ The Renaissance had literature.

What Was the Renaissance in Italy?

The Renaissance was a time for **art**.

▲ The Renaissance had art.

Chapter 2

What Were the Changes in Italy?

Italy had new literature. Italy had literature people liked.

▲ New literature was in Italy.

Italy had new books. Italy had books people liked.

▲ New books were in Italy.

Chapter 2

Italy had new art. Italy had art about people.

▲ New art was in Italy.

Italy had art about life.

▲ New art was in Italy.

What Were the Changes in Italy?

Italy had art with light.

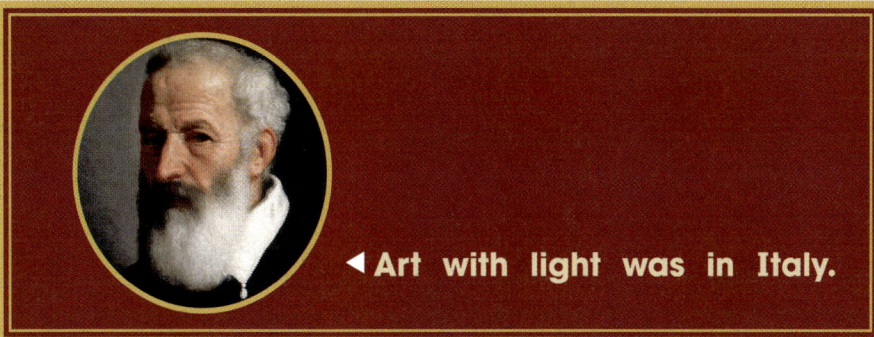
◀ Art with light was in Italy.

Italy had art with shadows.

▲ Art with shadows was in Italy.

Italy had art that looked real.

◀ Art looked real.

Chapter 2

Italy had great artists.

▲ Leonardo da Vinci was in Italy.

Did You Know?

Leonardo da Vinci painted in Italy. Da Vinci painted the *Mona Lisa*.

Mona Lisa ▶

What Were the Changes in Italy?

Italy had great art.

▲ Great art was in Italy.

Chapter 3

What Was Life Like in Italy?

Italy had **city-states**. Italy had five important city-states.

▲ Five important city-states were in Italy.

Italy had leaders.

It's a Fact
Some leaders were nobles. Some leaders were from the church.

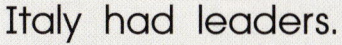
Leaders were in Italy.

Chapter 3

Italy had more businesses.

▲ New businesses were in Italy.

Italy had more rich people.

▲ Rich people were in Italy.

What Was Life Like in Italy?

Italy had **wars**.

▲ Wars were in Italy.

Conclusion

The Renaissance was in Italy. The Renaissance was a time for learning. The Renaissance was a time for art.

▲ Italy had learning. Italy had art.

Concept Map

The Renaissance in Italy

What Was the Renaissance in Italy?

a time
a time to study
a time to learn
a time for ideas
a time for literature
a time for art

What Were the Changes in Italy?

new literature
new books
new art about people
new art about life
new art with light
new art with shadows
new art that looked real
had great artists
had great art

What Was Life Like in Italy?

had city-states
had leaders
had more businesses
had more rich people
had wars

Glossary

art beautiful products that people make

*The Renaissance was a time for **art**.*

city-states cities and the land around them

*Italy had five important **city-states**.*

Italy a country in Europe

*The Renaissance was in **Italy**.*

literature written works

*The Renaissance was a time for **literature**.*

the Renaissance a time in European history

The Renaissance was a time in history.

wars fights between countries

Italy had wars.

Index

art, 7, 10, 13, 18

artists, 12

books, 9

businesses, 16

city-states, 14

history, 2

ideas, 6

Italy, 2, 4, 8–18

learning, 5, 18

life, 10

light, 11

literature, 6, 8

people, 8–10, 16

real, 11

Renaissance, the, 2, 4–7, 18

rich people, 16

shadows, 11

study, 5

wars, 17